Safety on Mou

Ten years have passed since the booklet **Safety on Mountains** was first published to help equip hill walkers with the skills essential for the enjoyment of the British mountains. Much like the original, this new edition of **Safety on Mountains** has been written for those venturing into the hills and onto the moors for the first time. But its scope does not stop there, the content goes beyond the basics and aims to help advise the hill walker as they develop skills applicable to all British mountain conditions. This new booklet expands the advice contained within the first **Safety on Mountains** booklet and updates advice on many new areas, such as modern clothing systems, GPS, mobile phones, and caring for the upland environment.

As more and more people discover the enjoyment of quiet, informal recreation in a special environment, hill walking has become more popular than ever before. With this rise in popularity, **Safety on Mountains** has become an increasingly valuable resource for the aspirant walker.

The title of **Safety on Mountains** should be clarified. No amount of reading, training or experience will make the hills 100% safe, they are a risky environment and you need to accept the possibility of mishaps before venturing out. What this booklet, coupled with learning and experience, can do is to help you understand the hazards and therefore minimise the risk. The vast majority of hill walkers enjoy a lifetime of the activity without ever having a serious incident, so perhaps a better title might have been '**Safer on Mountains**'.

Although this booklet goes into considerable detail on equipment and the mountain environment it is really a booklet about skills; examining and describing the full range of skills appropriate to both novice and seasoned walkers. All potential walking terrains are discussed, but rope skills are not within the scope of this booklet and are comprehensively dealt with in other publications. As well as defining the essential skills there are many training tips and ideas to help you convert this new found knowledge into practice.

Participation Statement

Hill walkers recognise that participation in all forms of hill walking is inherently risky.

You should only get involved if you are personally prepared to accept these risks and recognise that you will be exposed to potentially life-threatening situations.

BMC

Safety on Mountains

clothing – equipment – navigation – hazards – camping – environment – first aid

Photo – Courtesy of Scarpa

By purchasing this book, you are contributing to the BMC access and conservation work.

Safety on Mountains
Copyright © 2000 British Mountaineering Council

A British Library Cataloguing in Publication Data entry exists for this book.

ISBN 0 903908 271

Published by:
British Mountaineering Council,
177–179 Burton Road,
Manchester
M20 2BB

Designed, illustrated and typeset by Vertebrate Graphics, Sheffield.

ISBN 0 903908 271

9 780903 908276 >

Photo – Richard Heap

Hill walking is about being out in the hills and not just about bagging summits, so traversing a remote pass, crossing a wild moor, even walking some of the remote Scottish coastline, is just as much a part of this wild game.

chapter 1

What is hill walking?

Hill walking is an activity that takes the walker away from the confinements of the lowland track and up onto the higher moors and mountains. A hill walker's day could include considerable ascent and descent, possibly off well-trodden paths. As such, hill walking requires a degree of self-sufficiency, both in terms of equipment carried and of skills learned.

Where?

Britain is a country rich in mountain and moorland. Whilst the classic hill walking destinations of the Peak, North Wales, the Lake District, and Northern Scotland take pride of place, less well-trodden wild places such as Dartmoor, the Black Mountains, Northumberland and the Borders also offer great days out. Most areas will have a guidebook of one sort or another which describes the popular walking routes, but much of the enjoyment of a day out – and the purpose of this booklet – is to prepare you for planning and following your own route, taking you to your own points of interest.

In most walking areas there is plentiful accommodation, ranging from valley camping to expensive hotels and many will carry information specifically for walkers, such as suggested routes and weather forecasts.

So you want to go hill walking?

What do you need to have and what do you need to know? It is possible to have a great summer's day out in the hills with light clothing, comfortable footwear, a map and compass, some food and water and little else. This however makes the bold assumption that the weather will be good, and as any hill walker knows, winter conditions can be experienced during the summer months, and equally, mild summer conditions can occur during the winter months. For these reasons it is usual to take more equipment and this is all listed in the *Equipment* section on page 4.

The walker's key skill is navigation, including route-planning, and anyone venturing into the hills should be able to find their way around with confidence. Other walker's skills are subtle but essential, such as movement and general planning, these are also discussed in detail later on. The hills in winter conditions are an all together more serious matter and require an additional range of skills, which are explained in the *Winter Skills and Hazards* chapter on page 31.

The learning process: the next step?

Once you know what skills you need how do you go about gaining them? This booklet and the *Safety on Mountains* video will give you a grounding in the core skills, but book and video learning are no substitute for experience and practical learning. There are many ways of gaining practical skills. You may choose to go out with a more experienced friend, go out with a group from your local club, go on a course or simply learn from your own experience as you venture into progressively more challenging situations. Different approaches suit different people and various addresses are included in this booklet to help you make contact with the clubs, centres and resources that interest you – see *Further information* on page 49.

Whichever learning-path you choose, they all have one important aspect in common: skills alone are of little value and may even be dangerous unless they are linked with an appropriate amount of practical experience and the judgement that arises from it. As an illustration, the ability to take compass bearings from a map and pace distance accurately are valuable skills, but they could create a false sense of security if the walker had no experience of the potential severity of mountain weather and had never experienced walking through peat bogs before! Learning the skills is the easy part, but you cannot shortcut the process of gaining experience and judgement.

Photo – Courtesy of Craghoppers

How important is it to have good equipment?

chapter 2

Equipment

One of the great appeals of the British hills is that they are accessible to all and a great day out can be had with minimal equipment. There is not much that is vital, but there is plenty of gear that can make for a more pleasant day out if the conditions turn against you. What this chapter aims to do is identify the appropriate equipment and give some advice to help you choose the right kit. For each item of equipment we have covered only the most important points and much more will be found written on the subject elsewhere.

How important is it to have good equipment? It is important to realise that equipment, skills and experience all combine to equip the walker for days on the hill. All three should be developed together and possibly the least important is the equipment. Good equipment and poor decision making is clearly a potentially more dangerous combination than having poor equipment, but making good decisions.

N.B. *Camping equipment is discussed later in the* Camping in the Hills *chapter on page 37.*

Recommended

Summer conditions

- Comfortable boots and socks
- Waterproofs – jacket and trousers
- Map and compass
- Rucksack (small for day walks, large for multi-day)
- Food and drink
- Spare food
- Headtorch and fresh battery
- Hat/gloves/scarf/fleece

Personal or at least one amongst a group

- Whistle
- First aid kit
- Emergency bivvi bag
  (for example, bothy bag, poly bag)

Winter conditions

The above plus:

- Crampons
- Ice axe
- Gaiters
- Warm clothing, and spares including hat and gloves (see *Clothing systems* on page 7)

Very useful

Summer conditions

- Gaiters
- Sunhat
- Sunglasses
- Map case or laminated map
- Spare socks
- Trekking poles
- Sunscreen (potentially essential)
- Insect repellent (could be vital)
- High-energy food

Winter conditions

The above (except insect repellent and maybe sunhat) plus:

- Thermos flask
- Bivvi bag/bothy bag
- Goggles
- Balaclava

Potentially useful aids

- Global Positioning System
- Mobile phone
- Altimeter

Summer conditions

Boots

If your boots are not comfortable, you are going to have a miserable day. Fortunately the number and variety of boots on the market means that you should be able to find a comfortable pair.

Some advice:

- Decide whether you are looking for a light summer boot, a winter boot or an all rounder? As a general principle, go for the lightest pair that will do the job. Walking in heavier boots than are required involves a lot of extra work, but may provide more protection and greater foot and ankle support.

- Take time and shop around. A good retailer will be able to offer you plenty of advice on which to base your choice.

- Try the boots on with your own socks. Specialist walking socks have design features that affect the fit of your boot, so bear this in mind when selecting your boot size. A good fit will give you room around the toes whilst holding the heel so that it doesn't lift too much.

- Some boots, particularly fabric ones, are available with waterproof, breathable linings. Considering the generally damp British conditions, such a lining could be a worthwhile investment.

- Many shops will let you take the boots home for a few days' indoor trial and then let you return them if they're not quite right.

- Ankle support comes from having a good firm sole-construction with heel cups to hold the ankle in place. Boots without a cupping heel are not going to give as good support.

- Sole-construction can vary from rugged but soft-soled, to insensitive and rigid. These perform differently in different conditions. Expected use and personal preference will determine which you buy. For example a soft sole bends to conform to the shape of the surface while a rigid sole gains grip by locking onto small edges and so on.

Having bought the boots go for a few short walks before embarking on the 'big one'. This will soften up the boot and make you aware of any rub points and the best socks to fit. The stiffer and heavier the boot, the more breaking in will be required. If you do feel the boots rubbing uncomfortably on your foot, stop and apply tape or a plaster; this will prevent misery and blisters later. Check the manufacturer's instructions for advice on care. At the end of the day your boots will be damp; allow them to dry slowly and don't be tempted to put them too close to the fire.

Winter boot
High-cut to give ankle protection
Square-cut heel
Stiff sole
Welt for clip-on crampons

All-rounder
Welt for crampons
Square-cut heel
Leather upper
Slightly curved sole

Summer shoe
Light, breathable upper
Inside heel cup to give ankle support
Well-featured sole to give good grip

Boot soles

Insoles and midsoles: The insole is also known as the footbed and is likely to be removable. A good insole will give some cushioning. If you want improved cushioning or need to change the fit, then you could try fitting a shock-absorbing insole.

The midsole usually consists of two parts: a plastic or nylon layer is designed to give graduated stiffness appropriate to the type of boot; a good boot will also have a further shock-absorbing layer in the midsole.

Outsole: The sole of a boot is a very technical item and a lot of design work goes into getting the right combination of grip and durability. A large proportion of hill walking accidents are due to a simple slip and so the importance of having an effective boot sole cannot be overstated. Boot soles are designed with particular uses in mind, so buy a model that fits your requirements. Remember also that the boot's effectiveness will be reduced as the sole wears. So resole early and don't wait until the pattern is gone. A final point: to be effective a boot needs to be used properly, this is where movement skills come in and their importance should not be undervalued.

The rucksack

Most keen walkers will own at least two sacks. A small one for the short days out and a large one for multi-day walks. For a day walk a 30–40 litre sack is quite adequate and need not be overly complex.

A sack for multi-day use is likely to be 60–75 litres in capacity and as it will probably be carrying more weight, you should take care to buy one that fits your back well. Packs will have either fixed-length or adjustable-back systems. A good pack which fits well will have a substantial padded waist belt that allows you to take the majority of the weight on your hips, with the shoulder straps giving extra support and stability.

A good sack will also:

- be water resistant;
- have accessible pockets;
- have compression straps;

- have a sturdy hard wearing construction with solid zips;
- have a padded back, ideally ribbed or featured to circulate air.

Packing tips*:

- Keep small regularly used items in the top pocket.
- Line the sack with a bin bag or similar to ensure water proofing.
- Pack thinking about the order in which you are going to need things. Distribute weight evenly.
- Keep the sack as light as possible and don't take unnecessary luxuries.

* *Be aware manufacturers litre measurements vary greatly, one 70ℓ sack may be much bigger or smaller than another so make sure you get the right size for your needs.*

Compass

For most navigational needs a relatively simple compass is perfectly adequate. With a compass it is a case of *'it's not what you've got, it's how you use it'*, however those on a baseplate, with Romer scales which directly show distance are extremely useful.

Map

Britain is covered by maps in fantastic detail and 1:50 000, 1:40 000 and 1:25 000 scale maps offer a wealth of information. For areas that you walk in regularly, it is worth laminating or waterproofing your map to protect it from the rain. You can also buy pre-laminated maps. Since many maps cover a much greater area than you are ever likely to walk in, it may also be worth cutting your maps down to size.

Clothing systems

You can spend a tremendous amount of money on a clothing system that will keep you warm and relatively dry in the most severe conditions. You can spend a lot less money on clothes that will keep you adequately warm and dry in most conditions. The decision is yours, but you do not need to spend a fortune to have a good, reasonably comfortable day out. For many a summer walking day you simply need light comfortable clothing whilst you walk, something warm for when you stop and light waterproofs in case of a downpour.

The key clothing items are the waterproofs or windproofs. These come in breathable and non-breathable varieties. Non-breathables are cheap and robust, but as they don't let perspiration escape, they can become increasingly uncomfortable as the day wears on.

Breathables come in many varieties and prices, and will be made of either laminated or coated fabrics. Costs range from relatively cheap to very expensive and most walkers feel the added comfort to be well worth the price. When buying look out for the following desirable features:

Jacket

- Big enough to get plenty of layers under but not so big it flaps around.

- Pockets which ideally allow access without undoing the front of the jacket.

- Stiffened hood which gives good visibility when up, but which can be fixed out of the way when not in use.

- Durability in both the fabric and the waterproofing.

- Good closures at the wrist.

Trousers

- Good freedom of movement without being too flappy in the wind.

- Can be put on whilst wearing boots or even crampons.

Baselayers

Designed to wick perspiration away from the body and so prevent cooling by evaporation. This helps to prevent excessive chilling when you stop for a breather.

Insulation

To layer or not to layer?

The layering system is currently prevalent. The idea being that the insulation comes from a number of layers (typically thermal, fleece/pile, duvet, windproof) which can be added or discarded depending on the temperature and conditions. The system gives flexibility and can cope with the coldest conditions. The alternative is the single-layer system. Here an insulating fibre pile is combined with a pertex windproof shell to give a single garment, worn next to the skin, that keeps you warm by wicking moisture away from the body as quickly as possible, whilst relying on good ventilation to cool the body in hot conditions. This system has many devotees and is cheaper and more hassle-free than the layering system. Its weakness is perhaps at the extremes of the temperature range. In the coldest conditions more layers will need to be added and in the hottest weather an alternative is going to be preferred.

Socks

Good socks are worth the money and there is many a time when a spare pair will make a big difference. Good socks will both insulate and ventilate the foot, protect it from abrasion and provide some shock absorption. You may hear the phrase sock-shoe system; this serves to remind the walker that the fit of the boot is dependant on the sock and comfort is dependant on both.

Gloves

These need not be over-specialised. A simple pair of woollen gloves (or mittens which are warmer) is likely to be fine. As with socks a spare pair weighs very little but at times can be vital. Gloves that retain warmth even when wet are a real advantage. These could be thick woollen ones, windproof fleece or a waterproof outer glove and so on.

Gaiters

Gaiters stop snow and, to a certain extent, water from getting into the boot. Used in summer during very wet weather and when crossing boggy ground, they come into their own in winter conditions.

Standard gaiters cover the top part of the boot and lower leg. They will keep snow out but are not entirely waterproof and provide little insulation. Standard gaiters are available in many materials but the simplest will do the job perfectly well. The under-boot fixing should be of a durable material and can be replaced with a wire to extend gaiter life.

Supergaiters cover the whole boot and lower leg, a rubber rand seals the base tightly around the boot. Whilst being very good at keeping snow and water out and keeping the feet warm, supergaiters are expensive and only stay attached on quite stiff boots unless adhesive is used.

Headwear

A sun hat for the sun and a balaclava for when it gets cold. Believe it or not, sunstroke can be a real problem on the British hills, and a good hat (and plenty of liquid) will make all the difference. In cold conditions a tremendous amount of heat will be lost through the head, a balaclava will reduce this. Lightweight and waterproof fleece caps provide a comfortable alternative which can replace both balaclava and hood. Protecting the neck from the wind will also reduce heat loss.

Bivvi bag

Your shelter when you need to get out of the wind and rain. It could be a large polythene bag, which is cheap but rather unpleasant, a purpose made 'bothy bag' or survival unit. In serious conditions the breathable bags have considerable advantages and a light compact bothy bag, kept in the bottom of your pack 'just in case' would seem a wise investment.

Trekking poles

Increasingly common, these are a variation on ski poles and serve to reduce impact on the knees and improve balance. They are particularly useful when carrying a heavy sack, but like all other equipment, require thought as to how best they can enhance your mountain day. Too short and they do not

Trekking poles – research suggests that using two is better than one, especially with a heavy sack.

provide support, too long and they can trip you up. They can be packed away for sections of rocky terrain or scrambling.

Sunscreen

Serious sunburn is by no means unlikely on a summer's day in the high hills. A good strong sunscreen is an essential piece of kit in these conditions. For most sunny days, a waterproof sunscreen with a sun-protection factor (SPF) of 10 or more, plus lip-salve, would be appropriate. Good practice is to apply the cream in advance – and always remember that in a cooling wind the effects of the sun are easily underestimated.

Insect repellent

Despite its diminutive size, the Scottish midge is one of the most vicious creatures on earth, making strong repellent essential in the summer season. DEET is the standard ingredient in repellents. It is highly effective but is powerful and potentially harmful. The repellents with high concentrations of DEET need to be used with care and kept away from children. If you are planning to be out for a long period it would seem wise to use a relatively low concentration repellent (50% or below). Good natural alternatives to DEET exist and you should experiment to find what works for you.

Eye protection

Sunglasses can be useful in both winter and summer. In severe winter conditions goggles will be preferred as they protect the eyes better from wind-blasted snow. Good sunglasses will cut out UV light and you should check the filtering properties before you buy. If you wear eyeglasses then take a spare pair, a small tumble could otherwise turn into a disaster. Contact lenses are obviously easier to use than glasses in heavy precipitation, but not all spectacle wearers are able to use lenses.

Food and drink

As crucial, perhaps more so, as having the right equipment is having sufficient food and drink. The amount of food and drink required by the body will vary depending on conditions, distance and terrain walked. On a warm summer's day you can get away with a small amount of food but will suffer if you

skimp on the drink. On a cold winter's day you need a good quantity of food and drink to keep warm and a hot drink is likely to be very welcome. Before the walk, a good breakfast will set you up well and on the way little and often is best and it is sensible to have an emergency chocolate/energy bar or two tucked out of the way, just in case. It would be easy to get over-technical about calorie intake and balanced diets. Unless you plan to be on the go for weeks then you should go for the snack food that you enjoy.

In the case of drinks, water will do the job perfectly well, but you do need to be careful when taking water from streams. In theory running water without farm or habitation upstream should be fine but in recent years there have been increasing reports of pathogens such as giardia being found in previously clean streams. This is probably due to wild camping and poor waste-management. If you know you will be drinking stream water – when camping for example – it is worth boiling the water and/or carrying Iodine tablets. A hot drink in winter can help make you feel good, although the extra calorific value is minimal. If you are going to buy a flask then a hard wearing stainless steel model is going to be worth the extra money.

It is usually wise to boil stream water before drinking it.

Mobile phones

It is increasingly common for walkers to take their phones into the hills and there is no doubt that on occasions phones have saved lives. However several key points must be stressed:

- Using a phone to **a:** ask for directions, **b:** ask for additional food and clothing to be brought to the user, **c:** ask to be rescued for a non-life-threatening or disabling injury, is rightly considered as an abuse of the technology. Mountain rescue teams have identified abuse of mobile phones as a major problem and one which could severely limit their ability to respond to genuine emergencies.

- If a phone is to be carried it should in no way be allowed to influence the plan for the day. Walkers carrying a phone should not be tempted to push on further or to attempt objectives that they would normally consider outside their experience or ability. A mobile should not distort the essential principle of self-reliance. The hills offer the opportunity to be alone and fully-dependent on your own abilities. If you would not go out without the mobile, then you should seriously consider whether you are doing the right thing.

- A mobile phone is an emergency backup and is not a device that in itself increases your safety.

- A mobile phone is not a reliable communication device in the mountains and large parts of mountainous Britain have no coverage.

GPS

The GPS (Global Positioning System) is based on 24 orbiting satellites operated by the US military. It is a navigational aid that can provide a lot of useful information but it is also important to remember that it does not replace a map and compass. In theory a hand-held GPS can give a positional accuracy of ±1m. In practice the accuracy is a little less than this and more importantly the US military has selectively degraded the signal, such that for 5% of the time the accuracy can be as poor as ±300m. This uncertainty has severely limited the usefulness of the GPS as a navigational aid in the hills where complex terrain demands much greater navigational accuracy. In addition the GPS is a line-of-sight device and may not work in deep valleys or trees. If it cannot 'see' enough sky to get a fix on at least three satellites it will not give a reading.

In the near future, competing satellite-based navigational systems will come on line and it is likely that the US will stop degrading the GPS signal. This will lead to a genuine ±1m accuracy. This will not solve the line-of-sight problem. Despite this we can expect that a satellite positioning system will become a common component of the walkers kit list. As already stated such systems are a very useful tool but not a stand-alone one. To use one effectively you must already be able to accurately interpret a map and navigate with a compass. A satellite system without a map and compass is of little use in the hills, nor is it of any use when the batteries have run down.

Winter equipment

You will require more substantial outer clothing for winter walking. The winds tend to be stronger and precipitation (even) more frequent, putting greater demands on your clothes and making it more difficult to stay warm and dry. In addition to more clothing you will need several items of specialist equipment if venturing onto the hills in winter conditions. Before going out it is worth noting that winter conditions can occur on the British hills virtually all year round. Accidents in autumn and spring are common, where walkers equipped for a summer hike meet snow or ice on the ground and/or get caught in blizzards. When accidents occur in the mountains the casualties are almost always suffering from some degree of hypothermia, and so appropriate clothing, plus spares, is a key component of the winter kit list. Winter walking requires additional skills such as *self arrest*, *avalanche-* and *cornice-awareness*, *crampon movement skills* and very accurate *navigation*. These skills are all discussed elsewhere and this chapter will simply describe the equipment.

Ice Axes

A typical walkers axe is pictured. Note the shape of the head and pick. The shallow angle of the pick allows for smoother braking when compared with a technical climbing axe. Walkers axes are relatively long, typically over 55cm. Many walking axes are bought without a wrist leash. There are pros and cons to adding one. On the plus side a wrist loop protects against accidental dropping or loss during self arrest. On the negative side it will interfere as the axe is passed from hand to hand whilst zig zagging up or down a slope. It is important to keep the axe in the 'uphill hand' when zig-zagging, you must decide whether a leash improves or interferes with your safety.

Crampons

Crampons are used for travel over hard-packed snow or ice. It is essential to buy crampons which are compatible with your boots, so take your boots with you when you go shopping. The compatibility chart below will be helpful and full fitting details are found in the BMC's *Crampons Technical Booklet*.

Boot/crampon compatibility

Boots

B0: Not recommended for crampons.

B1: Suitable for the easiest snow and ice conditions found when hill walking. Crampons likely to be used in an emergency of when crossing short sections of snow or ice.

B2: A stiff flex boot designed for mountain use and could be used all day with crampons.

B3: A technical climbing/mountaineering boot. Rigid.

Crampons

C1: A flexible walking crampon attached with straps. With or without front points.

C2: Articulated multi-purpose crampons with front points. Attached with straps all round or straps at the front and clip on heel.

C3: Articulated or fully rigid technical crampon attached by full clip-on system at toe and heel.

B3 boots are ideal for C3 crampons and will take C2 and C1 crampons. At the other end a B1 boot could only be recommended with a C1 crampon.

Photo – Courtesy of Craghoppers

Prior to detailing the key hill walkers skills it would seem sensible to remind ourselves why those skills are required, that is, by discussing hazards and identifying some of the ways in which the risks they pose can be reduced. The practice of assessing hazards and considering how they might be minimised is known as risk assessment and this is a key part of the planning of a good day out.

Mountain weather

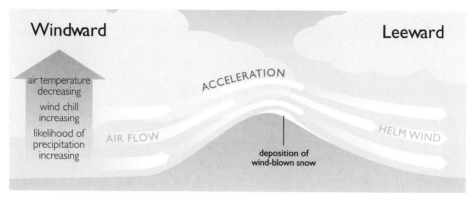

Air flow accelerates over a mountain barrier. This is a result of it being squeezed between the mountain top and the ceiling created by a warm frontal surface.

The weather will have a massive impact on your day. Weather in the mountains can be very different to that at sea-level and the consequences of being caught out in unexpected conditions can range from uncomfortable to desperately serious. Not only should hill walkers develop their understanding of the typical weather systems that affect the UK, but they should also understand how to interpret a sea-level forecast for the mountain environment. In addition to this understanding is the crucial connection that must be made between forecast weather conditions and how this will feel in practice. It is all very well knowing that the wind speed at 1000m, for example, will be 45mph from the south west – but knowing how this will impact upon your plans, and what alternatives to the planned day might be viable, is also important.

Some important points to bear in mind about mountain weather:

- Air is compressed as it flows over mountain regions. This means that wind speed will increase as you go higher. What feels like a stiff breeze in the valley can become a gale on the summit ridge and may make the going a lot harder than expected. Typically you will need to multiply the sea-level wind speeds by 2–3 times to estimate the wind speed on an exposed mountain top.

- Air temperature decreases with altitude, typically at a rate of about 1°C per 100m. In addition wind chill will lower the effective temperature. The drop in effective temperature is dependent on the wind speed and the air temperature. The effects of wind chill are mitigated by wearing windproof clothing.

- It can also be much wetter. The mountains encourage precipitation, so it is always wise to be prepared.

- The increased severity of mountain weather can have another effect. Cold, rain and wind will together create a sense of anxiety and urgency. This can lead to hurried and unconsidered decisions being made. Good planning will predict the likelihood of these conditions and allow some critical decisions to be made in advance. Practising navigational skills will also make the process quicker. Whatever the case, a moment to double-check is likely to be well spent.

- Wind direction is also an important factor. In winter conditions it dictates where wind slab (avalanche conditions) will form. Wind direction should be considered at all times when planning your route. Having a strong wind at your back when up high is going to be much quicker and more comfortable than fighting against it.

- British mountains are affected by mist and low cloud. This means that on all but the clearest days there is a chance of encountering very poor visibility. This reinforces the need for good navigational skills.

- It is important to remember that it is possible to encounter snow and ice virtually throughout the year. This possibility needs to be taken into account when route planning.

- Hot conditions can also cause problems. Sunstroke and dehydration are exceedingly debilitating. For hot summer days, take plenty of liquid and sun-protection.

- Weather forecasts will always be better understood if you can build up a picture of how the prevailing weather has built up over time. Developing a knowledge of the weather systems that affect the UK, how they move and what conditions they bring with them, will also help your understanding of the forecast.

Experience and understanding of weather, paying attention to forecasts, being ready for abrupt changes, being well equipped and, of course, being able to navigate if caught out, all go some way toward reducing then risks posed by Britain's weather.

For further information see '*Weather for hill walkers and climbers*' by Thomas and for sources of weather information see *Further information* on page 49.

Hazards of steep ground
Steep grass slopes

The most common cause of serious accidents in the mountains in the UK is a simple slip. When involved in technical and demanding hill walking, it is usual to be very focused on the challenges at hand, but when on easier ground it is tempting to relax and lose concentration. Steep grass slopes can be extremely hazardous – not only in wet conditions, but also when the grass is long and dry. Walkers should be aware that it is not the ground underfoot that defines the seriousness of a situation, but the consequences if a fall occurs. An unbroken steep grassy slope may well be far more serious than a steeper, but short rocky slope.

Ascent/descent/traversing

Steep ground is always easier to *ascend* in control than it is to *traverse* or *descend*. You should always know how you are going to get back down a mountain before you start to climb. If it is a steep slope, then this will be both more time-consuming and more difficult than expected. In ascent the ground ahead is close to you and your steps are shorter, foot placements are easy to spot and leaning into the slope will add to the sense of security. In contrast, during descent you need to extend downwards for each step, placements are more difficult to settle on and you will need to lean out to improve the security of your foot placements. Clearly, practice in secure places, on short slopes, with safe run-outs will help you develop the judgement you need.

Hidden hazards

When looking either up or down a concave slope you will be able to see the whole length of it. However a convex slope curves in such a way that your horizon hides what is beyond, which effectively means you will be walking into the unknown. On ascent this may simply be frustrating, because you may find an impasse which requires a return to your starting point and to try again. In descent, a convex slope may hide real dangers such as a line of cliffs, an uncrossable river, a horribly steep grass slope, a snow patch or a boundary fence. Learn to recognise convex slopes from the map and beware of their hazards.

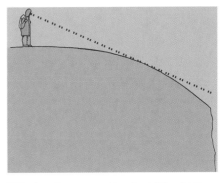

Hidden hazards – a convex slope will cut off line-of-sight from potential danger.

Scree

Scree – loose surface rocks – is a facet of mountain walking which will be encountered on many occasions. Due to the unstable nature of scree, it is often tiring to ascend (2 steps forward, one step back), but fast to descend (running with the flow as the scree slides down the hillside). In certain wet conditions, scree can be extremely unpleasant to cross – being both unstable and slippery, and care should be taken. As with any skill, however, practice can improve performance and it is worth concentrating, particularly on foot placements, to maximise the security that can be found. **Please note:** Scree running is environmentally damaging as it accelerates erosion.

Rocks

Although it is often tempting to scramble on rocks when climbing mountains, the potential hazards of this should be borne in mind. What would be the consequences if you fell? Is it easy to reverse back down again and is there an easy way off the top? What would be the consequences for other mountain walkers if you knocked a rock off on top of them?

Scrambling is a hazardous practice and involves a whole new set of movement skills, and familiarity with the appropriate protection techniques.

People

Walkers moving over scree or loose rocky ground are prone to dislodging rocks onto those below. Be aware of this and keep out of fall lines if possible.

Good movement skills, concentration, forward thinking and an understanding of the map are needed to move safely over slippery slopes and other difficult terrain.

Water hazards
(including marshes, streams and rivers)

As an island, the UK has a high rainfall, and much of this is concentrated in the mountain areas. Consequently water hazards are continually changing in seriousness and any keen mountain walker should be aware of the risks associated with

Mountain streams can become raging torrents very quickly.

a crossing. Marshy areas can be extremely deep and a fall into one can bring about serious discomfort, if not actually posing a threat to life. Maps will show where a marsh may be present and experience will let a walker identify a deep marsh from the terrain and type of vegetation present – a skill that can help a lot with the enjoyment of a day on the mountain.

Mountain streams high on a hillside can become raging torrents in a very short period of time. Both spring thaw and heavy rainfall can cause a stream to rise very quickly, but the positive counter to this is that they also fall equally quickly. Whereas rivers pose a clearly identifiable threat which can generally be avoided, mountain streams have to be crossed frequently – so judgement must be developed about when a stream crossing becomes an unacceptable risk. Caution is the right approach here: plan to avoid crossing water hazards in wet or thaw conditions and if in doubt about the wisdom of a crossing, don't do it! Remember that a valley river will take longer to rise in poor conditions, but will also take longer to fall. With a reliable weather forecast, most water-related hazards can be predicted. The seriousness of water hazards differs greatly from one mountain region to another – it is rarely necessary to cross them in most mountain regions of England and Wales, but water hazards can be a problem in Scotland where there are fewer crossing options. Drownings do occur, so when planning a day, very serious consideration must be given to avoiding potentially dangerous crossings. Study your map and monitor the weather before deciding on your route.

Water hazards: crossing techniques

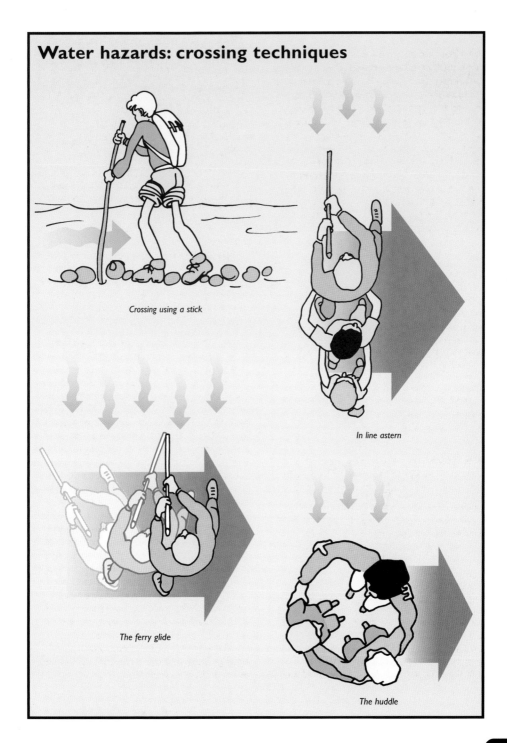

Crossing using a stick

In line astern

The ferry glide

The huddle

Unlike many other mountain walking skills, dealing with water hazards is not a skill area that should be practiced. In most cases, crossing a river or serious spate stream would be an emergency action rather than a part of a planned day. The sensible action is to avoid crossings and if you do have to do one, always make it the last resort.

Water hazards: crossing techniques

There are various unroped techniques that can be used to improve your stability when crossing streams and rivers which are worth thinking about in advance. The diagrams on page 17 illustrate a range of simple techniques – all based on the principles of maximising stability and security whilst minimising the surface area presented to the flowing water.
For further information see the *Plas y Brenin* booklet on the subject.

Winter hazards are dealt with later, along with winter skills.

hill walkers' skills

The skills needed by the hill walker can be summarised under the headings of *movement* (not slipping or falling over), *navigation* (not getting lost) and *planning and preparation* (being ready for what the mountain environment might throw at you). In general these skills are easy to acquire but time and practice are required so that they can be used with confidence. This chapter looks first at the core, year-round skills whilst the following chapter considers the skills and hazards relevant to winter conditions.

chapter 4

The learning curve

As with all personal skills, there are several things you can do to accelerate your learning. Gaining experience is an essential factor, but by thinking before you go out and reviewing your experiences after you have been out, you will develop skills more quickly. This cycle of activity – planning – doing – reviewing – can take place in micro sessions – before, during and after a ten minute navigation leg – or on a larger scale – before, during and after a full mountain day.

Include other people in your planning, doing and reviewing as they may challenge your own perceptions and help you to develop more quickly. When all you really want to do is get out there in the hills and have a good time, stopping to think and analyse may seem rather uninteresting. If you are keen to venture further afield than you have done before, it is definitely worth developing your skills at least as fast as you extend your experience. However, you should never need to let planning and reviewing interfere with the joy of the doing.

Movement skills

It is worth repeating: *the majority of accidents in the hills are the result of the simple slip or stumble.* It follows that good footwork and concentration will result in a safer day out. What do we mean by good footwork? Firstly how do we keep our footing?

Friction: Friction depends on both the rubber of the sole of your boot and the surface being walked on. Generally the more of the boot sole in contact with the ground the greater the friction. On very slippery ground it may not be possible to maintain footing by friction alone, this is where grip and edge come into it.

Grip: The grip results from the shape of the boot sole and, as already stated, it is important to have a sole which is appropriate to the terrain and in good condition.

Edge: On slippery ground the edge of the boot will have to be used to get purchase. Often on grass and certainly on snow (but not ice) this will involve kicking into the ground to get a placement.

Needless to say a rigid boot will help this process whereas a soft soled boot or shoe will not be able to edge effectively.

Once again it is practice, in safe places, which will allow you to get a feel for how your boots perform in varying circumstances.

Good footwork means using your footwear effectively and maintaining concentration so as not to be caught out by a slippery surface (grass, lichen, verglas…), loose rock, or an unstable block. The need for concentration means that you should try to avoid hurrying, especially in descent. It also means maintaining balance with the weight over the feet. Leaning back in descent or forward in ascent will increase the likely hood of a slip.

Negotiating steep ground

When faced with a rocky, boulder-strewn hillside, being able to choose a good route through and a realistic understanding of your own or your party's capability are judgements that must be developed.

The mountains of the UK include much steep and rocky terrain which goes beyond walking and requires *scrambling* skills. The full range of scrambling skills and the appropriate protection techniques are beyond the scope of this booklet. However on many hill walks you will find short sections of steep, rocky ground that are unavoidable and need to be negotiated. In such cases take your time to ensure you are taking the best route and be aware of loose or slippery rock. Empty your hands and if unsure then face in, take your time and use your hands (now you are scrambling). Keep looking ahead and try to keep on the best line, this is very important. On short sections of steep ground, members of a party can watch out for each other (*spotting*) and be ready in the event of a slip.

As with all steep ground, it feels far more secure and is usually easier to select a good line in ascent compared with descent. If you have any doubt whatsoever about your ability to complete an ascent it is advisable to get into the habit of looking down over the ground you have just ascended. Can you get back down if you need to? Don't go up what you can't climb down.

Navigation

Without being able to navigate you are restricted to way marked paths. Maps provide the key to being able to develop the skills of a competent mountain navigator, and with a compass the combination should enable a walker to soon be in control of their destiny in the mountains. Additional navigational tools such as a GPS may assist with tracking location, but do not reduce the importance in any way of developing good map and compass skills. The first step to confident navigation is to understand the map. Get to know the map well before trying to use the compass.

Maps

Maps provide all the detail you need to plan a route away from paths, to identify potential alternatives and to make sensible responses to changing circumstances. Maps can be used to identify your position and find a route across a mountain range, but they also do much more to enhance the enjoyment of your trip.

Although 1:25 000 maps are available for most mountainous areas of the UK, smaller scale maps such as 1:40 000 and 1:50 000 are also perfectly adequate. In some ways the smaller scale maps make planning and route finding easier because they convey the ground shape without a lot of additional superficial information. The larger scale maps are easier to use when navigating in complex areas such as the margins of open country where walls and fences abound, and where detailed micro-navigation is essential.

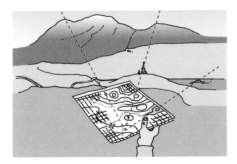

Setting a map by reference to identifiable features on the ground. The feature, its map position and your eye must all occupy the same vertical plane.

A knowledge of map reading is essential in the mountains.

Grids, scales and distance

All maps have the grid-line system imposed upon them. These grids represent one-kilometre squares regardless of the map scale and can be used as a useful rough measure when planning a route.

When you know the scale of a map you can use a measuring scale usually found on the base of a compass to measure the distance between two points and convert this to a distance on the ground. It is good to develop a knowledge of quick-conversions without having to think – such as 1cm = 250m (1:25 000) and 2mm = 100m (1:50 000). A Romer scale on the compass baseplate will translate directly for each given map scale.

Land shape

Paths, fences, streams and roads can all change shape or be re-routed, so the most reliable information a map can give you is the shape of the land itself. This is conveyed by contour lines which, with practice, can be seen to illustrate ridges, valleys, flat land and even small undulations and so on. Be aware that different maps use different contour intervals, which in particular can change the apparent steepness of a slope.

Preparing and carrying the map

It is extremely helpful to carry your map in a way that helps you to use it. It should be:

Compact: folded or cut to size so that the area you need is visible and the area you do not need is out of sight or left at home!

Accessible: stored ready to use in a jacket pocket, a map needs to be looked at without interrupting your walk.

Customised: by cutting or folding it to size and weather-proofing – a small, hand-held map which doesn't get soggy is easy to orientate and therefore better for keeping track of the features around you.

Orienting the map

Orienting or *setting the map* means that you match the map to the terrain. So if you are facing the south, the map in your hand needs to be upside down if the features on the map are to match the terrain as you see it. By orienting the map, ground features fall into place and your ability to visualise the detail drawn on the map will begin to develop.

To get better at map reading you need to combine outdoor experience with study of the relevant map.

The following will help you understand the information within the map:

During a walk, get in the habit of checking the details on your map at regular intervals even if you don't actually need to be navigating at the time. By comparing what actually exists outdoors with how this is shown on a map you will develop your ability to do the reverse process – that is, use the map to plan a walk.

Reflect on a walk in the comfort of an armchair by tracing your route over the map and comparing the real experience with the map picture. What does that steep ascent actually look like on the map? How is that craggy edge illustrated?

Build on your experience of previous trips to help you plan in detail for the next one. Planning should be seen as an opportunity to increase the challenge and excitement of a trip as well as a means of reducing the risk and making it safer.

Compasses and other navigational aids

A compass enables the walker to identify direction accurately, which becomes a crucial skill when walking in poor visibility. If you can read and interpret a map well, then most of the time you will only need to use a compass to help orient the map correctly or to walk in an approximate direction

(that is, roughly north rather than south when faced with a path junction). However, in poor visibility (such as in cloud, mist or poor light) you may need to follow an accurate compass bearing because it is not possible to see and interpret the land features.

It is important to remember that when converting bearings from the map to the ground or vice versa, allowance must be made for the magnetic variation specific to that area.

For more information, see *Navigation: Fixing your position*, on page 24.

Magnetic variation

The *magnetic* pole is some distance to the west of the geographic pole and as a consequence your compass does not point to *grid* north. The difference between magnetic north and grid north depends on where you are in the world and it also varies over time. For the UK in 1999 Magnetic North was about 4° west of grid north and decreasing by about a degree every five years. Check on your map for the exact figure for the mountain area you are operating in. To convert from a magnetic bearing to a grid bearing you need to subtract the variation and vice versa.

The starting point for any navigational exercise is knowing where you are in the first place.

Locating position

Ideally, as you walk you will have been using the information provided by the map to keep track of your position. Inevitably though there will be times when you are not sure about where you are and so you need to relocate. The map and the ground you are on can provide you with the information to do this. The diagrams in *Navigation: Fixing your position* overleaf, suggest some ways of relocating your position in reasonable visibility.

Navigating in poor visibility

This is an essential skill and one which virtually all hill walkers are going to need at one time or another. The idea of navigating in zero visibility may appear daunting, but if you know where you started from (*locating position*), know which direction you are walking in (*walking on a bearing*), how far you have walked (*distance estimation*), then take into

Navigation: The compass

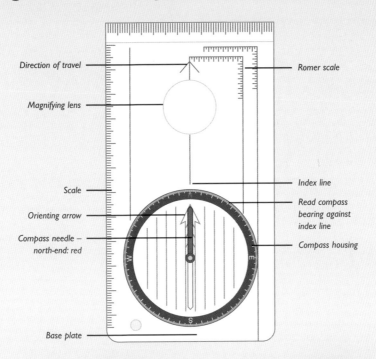

Direction of travel

Magnifying lens

Scale

Orienting arrow

Compass needle – north-end: red

Base plate

Romer scale

Index line

Read compass bearing against index line

Compass housing

Photo – Richard Heap

Navigation: Fixing your position

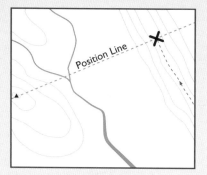

Using a transit to locate position on a ridge. When the stream junction and the peak are in line (transit) you will be at point X on the ridge.

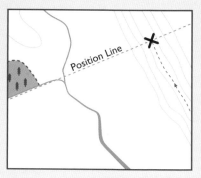

The edge of the forest or straight section of the stream provides a clue to your position on the ridge.

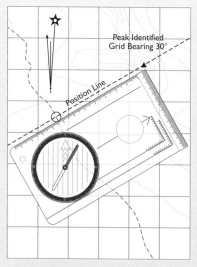

Using a back-bearing, having subtracted the magnetic variation to pinpoint position on a footpath.

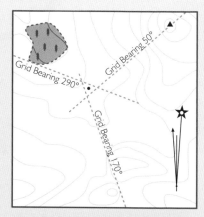

Using resection to find your position. Note the 'cocked hat' or triangle within which your position will lie.

account any factors that may induce errors, then you will reach your destination. When navigating in serious conditions it is crucial to have confidence in your navigational ability and so practice in less serious conditions is essential.

Practice for poor visibility situations by testing yourself in mist and at night in safe areas where you know basically where you are. Walking at night makes you focus on the essential skills – of direction, distance and land form underfoot – helping to build confidence in your ability to perform these techniques when really needed.

Walking on a bearing

First you must set the bearing on which you intend to walk. Lie the compass on the map with the edge in a line from your position towards the point where you want to be.

- Twist the housing until the orienting lines are parallel with the grid lines running north/south on the map.

- The bearing is the number on the housing that lines up with the compass direction of travel arrow.

- Add the magnetic variation (as you are transferring the bearing from map to compass).

- The bearing is now set.

For more information, see *Navigation: Taking a compass bearing from a map*, on page 26.

Once the bearing is set on the compass try holding it firmly against the base of your chest with the direction of travel arrow pointing forward. Then turn around until the floating magnetic needle is in line with the orienting arrow. By holding the compass in this way it ensures that your whole body is facing in the direction of travel which is the first stage in establishing the line of travel you will be following over the ground. This technique avoids the common problem caused by holding a compass out from the body pointing in the right direction, but at a slight angle from the body.

Next identify a few markers directly in line with the direction of travel arrow. Before beginning to walk try familiarising yourself with all the ground between where you are standing and the horizon by looking from your feet to the horizon and back again along the imaginary line you are about to walk. By doing this it may help you walk longer distances between stopping to check that you really are going in the right direction. If you think you may have strayed off line try turning round and aligning the wrong end of the magnetic needle with the orienting arrow in the compass – this way the direction of travel arrow will be pointing back to where you have just come from. Does it look familiar?

In poor visibility (such as cloud, darkness or blizzard conditions) markers such as distinctive boulders, patches of vegetation or changes in the terrain may not be visible. 'Leap-frogging' by sending one party member ahead to the limit of visibility and then catching up and repeating the process is effective, but slow. In severe conditions such techniques will not be possible and so you will be totally reliant on the map and compass. To be confident to do this you will have had to practice in less serious conditions. Once again it is a case of becoming comfortable with the skills before having to use them for real.

Some helpful navigational tools

Attack Points

When you are homing in on a small target such as the tent or snow hole you plan to spend the night in, Attack Point technique will help you maximise your chances of finding it first time. Rather than heading straight for your objective, go for the nearest well-defined target – such as a wall, ridge, stream junction and so on – and use this as a base to 'attack' your target. By approaching your destination like this, you will minimise the distance over which you need to do difficult navigation and if you do not find the target first time you can easily return to the attack point and start again.

Aiming Off

It is not the best idea to always aim directly at an objective when walking on a bearing in poor visibility. By doing so it is highly likely that errors will creep in, and you will end up to one side or the other of your target. If this happens you will not know which side you are on so it will be guess work to locate the objective. 'Aiming off' describes the technique of

Navigation:
Taking a compass bearing from a map

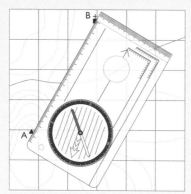

Step 1: *Place the long edge of the compass along the line of travel.*

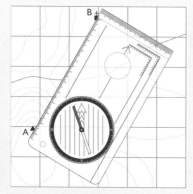

Step 2: *Turn the housing so that the orienting lines are parallel to the north/south grid lines.*

Step 4: *Now turn your body and the compass until the needle falls in the orienting arrow. Walk in the direction indicated by the travel arrow.*

Step 3: *Add the magnetic variation*

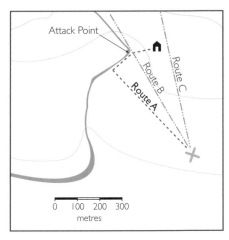

Aiming directly for the hut (Route C) is risky as a small error will mean missing it. Aiming instead for a distinct feature near the hut (Route B) from which to 'attack' the target makes more sense. Aiming off from the 'attack point', (Route A) makes sure you'll find it.

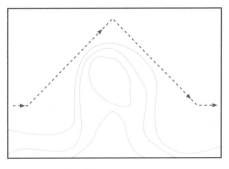

Avoiding a hazard by dogleg

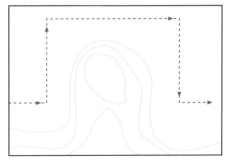

Avoiding a hazard by boxing

purposefully taking a bearing to one side and is most easily used when the objective is on or near a clear linear feature such as a stream, path, wall or ridge.

Avoiding hazards in poor visibility

Where a hazard exists which presents a real danger or is hard to cross – such as a cliff, cornice, swollen stream or avalanche prone slope – then you need a foolproof method of walking around it without losing your overall sense of direction. *Doglegs* and *boxing* are two easy techniques for doing this.

By doing a *dogleg* you simply go along two sides of a triangle rather than along the single long side. This will mean that you have travelled further, but the method will take you clear of the predicted hazard you identified on the map that was presenting an obstacle.

Boxing is also used when you have to avoid an obstacle when walking on a bearing. Instead of following a straight line route you walk around three sides of a box as shown in the illustration. This is achieved by walking to the side at +90° to the original bearing. Walk for a distance that is easy to remember (say 100m), next return to the main bearing for 100m, then walk for 100m on –90°.

Distance estimation

As important as the ability to walk on a bearing is the need to estimate accurately distance travelled. Pacing and timing are techniques that require practice in varied conditions before becoming an integral part of your personal 'toolbag' of skills. Pacing requires concentration and is best for short distances, say up to 500m. Whereas timing does not stop you from talking, thinking and route-finding and is suited to medium and longer length sections of the walk. Remember that you will need to be able to estimate distances going up, down and across slopes on grass, rocks or snow… so practice.

Identifying position in poor visibility

If you have become uncertain of your position in very poor visibility it can be difficult to relocate and so serious navigational errors may occur. It is therefore particularly important to keep track of position as visibility decreases. If uncertain of position the following may be helpful.

Slope aspect

The aspect of slope underfoot is often a useful piece of information to identify where you are. In whiteout conditions any sense of horizon is lost and it may be difficult to be sure whether you are travelling up down or across a slope. In winter, rolling a snowball can help you identify the *fall-line*, which is an imaginary line running straight down the hillside. On the map this line runs at 90° to the contour lines.

Establish the direction of the fall-line and take a compass bearing down it. Adjust this magnetic reading to a grid bearing and align the compass on the map until the housing is in line with the north/south grid lines and the edge is at 90° to the contours, this gives you a possible position line.

This technique does not give you an exact position, but it does provide an additional piece to the jigsaw by confirming which way the slope you are on is facing. Other useful pieces of information may be gleaned from the ground underfoot or even the wind direction. This process of narrowing down the options will hopefully allow you to walk on a bearing to a linear feature, which can then be followed to a fixed point. This is not an exact science so it's best not to get lost in the first place.

Some practical tips

Pacing: Take time to find out how many steps you take every 100m, as measured from the map. Do this on differing terrain. It may well be worth writing the results down.

Timing: There are various rules and formulas (Naismiths, Tranters corrections, and so on) that attempt to evaluate how long it will take for a walker to cover a given distance on various terrain. Whilst these give a general indication of how long a walk might take they are not 'personal' enough for accurate distance estimation. As with pacing you need to find out how long, at your normal pace, it takes you to cover a given distance. Again you need to do this over various terrain – flat, uphill, downhill, rocky, snow…

Errors

Winds:

Strong winds can push you off a bearing and affect the time it takes to cover a certain distance. It is key to be aware of the possibility and do your best to make adjustments.

Parallel errors:

The shape of the ground doesn't lie but it can lead you astray if you pick up a feature similar to that which you intended to follow. A typical example might be two broad parallel depressions. In the diagram below an initial error of a few degrees is being compounded and a serious situation could arise. You need to be aware of this possibility and use the information from your map and compass to avoid it.

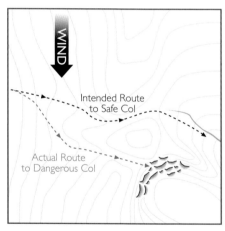

Parallel error. The strong north wind has caused the walker to drift south into a parallel feature which leads to the wrong col.

Rocky ridges

On very complex ground, the Cuillin ridge is a good example, the map and compass alone will not be enough to find your way and in poor visibility errors are easily made. If you don't have previous clear-weather knowledge of a particular ridge then you will discover the route-finding to be very difficult in bad weather, so beware.

Magnetic rocks

In some areas the local rocks are magnetised and so can induce compass errors, again the Cuillin is an example. Be aware of where such problems may occur and be prepared to navigate with the map alone.

Final tips

- Get the map out before you feel lost.

- Take advantage of windows of opportunity such as breaks in the cloud, single distinctive features or changes in the aspect of a slope continually to keep updated about your position.

- Keep a track in your mind of the terrain you have just crossed – this picture will help you confirm where you are in a way that a single 'snapshot' observation will not.

- Get others in the group to check navigation as well. This will minimise errors.

- Practice

Planning & preparation

A little planning and preparation can avoid a lot of difficulties later on.

It is hard to estimate exactly how many mountain incidents could have been avoided with better planning and preparation, but all would agree it's a lot.

Planning means selecting an objective that is appropriate to your fitness and skill level and then considering potential problems and hazards. Good preparation, with in-built flexibility, ensures we are equipped to deal with foreseeable problems.

With this in mind, consider how long the route will take, how forecast weather will affect it, how arduous it is likely to be – is it appropriate? What if the wind gets up and visibility drops? What escape options exist?

Consider risk areas such as potential avalanche slopes, cliffs, gullies or very complex terrain. In obviously complex, risky areas you may even feel the need to write down bearings and distances to lead you from a well-defined feature to your line

of descent. Think of the satisfaction as, in a snow storm as dusk is approaching, you find the winds are even stronger than expected as you begin to descend a summit ridge. Your less experienced partner is obviously struggling so you have to pretend that all is OK, despite the fact that you too are finding it hard going and have an urgent desire to be sitting by a fire at home. At this point because you planned in advance you can glance at a piece of paper with the crucial information written on it; 'from summit cairn; 68°, 350 metres'. This gets you out of the wind, morale and strength increase and your near epic becomes a controlled, positive and pub-talk-worthy experience. Without advance planning, the six minute dash on 68° would have been replaced with a five minute fumble with the map in strong winds in the dark with cold hands – before even beginning to move. Anxiety and uncertainty would have risen as you both got colder and in the stressful conditions there would be no guarantee that you would have come up with the best descent let alone an accurate measurement of the direction or distance.

Leaving route information

This means leaving an indication of your planned route with someone so that the alarm can be raised if you fail to return. This makes good sense but it is important that unnecessary call-outs be avoided. Therefore if information is to be left, it should be with someone who is able to understand it and make a judgement on how and when to act. Be careful when stating a return time and assume that delays will occur. Don't allow the fact you have left route information to fix your plans, be prepared to change your route once out on the hills if conditions dictate. If delayed don't feel forced to rush down over difficult ground so as to return at the time expected, a false alarm is better than an accident. Make sure that whoever the information was left with is informed that you have returned safely, especially if you did not follow your original plan. Too many rescue teams have been called out to look for people who were already safely at home but had forgotten to pass this fact on.

Photo – Richard Heap

The mountains in winter take on an altogether grander appearance and present a whole new set of challenges to the winter walker. There have been avalanches in October and cornice collapses in May, the days are short and the weather typically less stable. To meet these new challenges a range of new skills are required to supplement those gained during the summer. These skills are discussed here.

chapter 5

Winter skills and hazards

Winter conditions can occur in the mountains during almost any month of the year. This can be much more serious during the autumn if you are not properly prepared for it than in February when you have anticipated or are even hoping for such conditions. The importance of monitoring the weather before venturing into the hills and the need to know how to interpret a sea-level forecast into mountain conditions is obviously vital. Also, because the weather is unpredictable, it is important to know how to cope when conditions suddenly deteriorate. See *Mountain weather* on page 14 for details.

Winter walkers' skills are the same as mountaineering skills and it would be fair to say that in reality 'there is no such thing as hill walking in winter, there is only winter mountaineering'. To put this into perspective, in summer conditions the walk up Ben Nevis requires no more skills than those already described (and some people get away with having no skills or mountain sense whatsoever!). In winter conditions you need to be comfortable walking in crampons and know when to put them on, you need to be able to self arrest using an ice axe, you should have a feel for the potential severity of winter weather, know how to cope with it and be able to navigate in zero visibility with confidence. You need to be aware of the potential for avalanches and cornice collapse and be able to make some sort of judgement on the likelihood of either. The fact that the plants that grow on the mountain tops of the UK are those which you find in the Arctic and Alpine parts of the world illustrates the potential severity of the environment.

For a fuller discussion of winter hill skills, including climbing, see the **BMC Information Service: Winter Pack**.

Definitions:

Summer conditions:

Anytime except when winter conditions prevail. Any experienced mountaineer will be able to identify these conditions, but they don't just occur during the summer months.

Winter conditions:

This is when the following conditions either exist or are forecast: there is snow cover and/or the effective temperature is sub-zero, causing water to freeze. What is very important for the walker to realise is that this guiding principle should be applied to both the prevailing conditions *and* those forecast for the next 24 hours – illustrating the vital need to become familiar with good sources of weather information.

Winter weather

Weather has already been discussed in detail. In addition to lower temperatures, higher winds and more precipitation, you must add the fact that the ground underfoot will be frozen and icy, covered in snow or extremely boggy, and the days will be short – affecting both the hours of daylight and warmth conveyed by the sun.

All these elements must be taken into account as you plan your day. Get the best possible forecast, try and evaluate how this will translate into conditions on the mountains and consider how it will affect your planned route.

Avalanches

Although people associate big avalanches with Alpine areas, they do occur in Britain and they are the cause of fatalities. Although the causes of avalanches are complex and varied, the locations where they occur are relatively predictable. Being able to make a judgement on whether or not a slope is susceptible to avalanches is a key winter skill and until experienced and confident it is wise to be very cautious about crossing snow-laden slopes. In order for an avalanche to occur there needs to be a build-up of snow in the first place. Avalanches occur most often in lower-angled walkers'-terrain rather than the steeper slopes where climbers operate. This means that both climbers and winter walkers must be aware of the types of slope to avoid – whether it is in getting to and from a climb or up and down a mountain.

Types of avalanche

Loose snow (powder or wet): Initiated from a single point, can be tiny or massive depending on the amount of snow. They are usually caused by sheer weight of snow build up. Powder snow avalanches are very rare in Britain. Wet snow avalanches are usually associated with thaw conditions.

Slab (aka Wind Slab): The most common type of avalanches in the UK. A slab of snow detaches leaving a clear fracture line. They occur when one layer of snow (new, or most commonly wind-deposited) is weakly bound to the one below. Usually triggered by people walking into the unstable area. It is very important to realise that slab-avalanche conditions can occur during, immediately after, or several days after snowfall. This is because the conditions develop as a result of wind-blown snow being re-deposited on 'lee' (down-wind) slopes. Therefore as well as observation of conditions when you are out on the hill, the weather conditions (and particularly the wind direction and strength) in the preceding days determines whether slab avalanche conditions are likely.

Measurements are in centimetres

Slab test – indicates how firmly the surface layer is attached to the layer below

The following factors make an avalanche more likely:

The most common angle for an avalanche slope is 30°–45°. Slopes 20°–60° are however frequent sources of avalanches and this should be considered as the danger range. Avalanches from slopes outside this range are uncommon but not impossible. The following factors should also be considered:

- Fresh snow within last 24 hours
- Windy conditions depositing or re-depositing snow onto lee slopes
- Situations with a lack of bonding between layers such as fresh snow on top of an old icy layer, snow on wet grass, snow overlying smooth rock slabs.
- Thaw conditions

Although a single factor can cause an avalanche, serious avalanche conditions are likely if more than one of these factors exist.

Checking the slope:

Four useful ways to assess snow slope conditions are:

1. Appearance
2. The slab test
3. Recent weather history
4. Public Avalanche Information Services

Appearance: Wind blown snow typically has a chalky or creamy colour which can be seen from a distance. Other characteristics include a 'squeaky' noise when walked on. It is poor at forming snowballs!

Slab test: This tests the bonds between snow layers and is a good indicator of potential slab avalanche conditions.

Cornice

Defined as '*a consolidated snow bank projecting over the edge of a ridge, plateau or corrie, and formed by prevailing winds*'. Cornices are a serious winter hazard as they can collapse, either spontaneously as

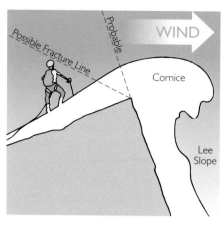

A cornice formation. Note possible fracture line. It is important to keep well back from the edge or the crest of the ridge.

temperatures rise (possibly causing an avalanche) or under the weight of a person (and so taking the person down with them). Cornices typically fracture some way back from the cliff/ridge edge and it is wise to keep well back from an edge unless you are absolutely sure there is no cornice. They are formed by the wind and generally occur on the lee side of the mountain from past or existing wind direction.

Weather history

Before venturing out into the hills, this information will help you work out which slopes are most likely to be prone to avalanches and where cornices might exist, therefore helping you plan to avoid exposing yourself to unnecessary risks.

Avalanche information

The Scottish Avalanche Information Service (SAIS) issues daily reports on snow conditions available from a variety of sources (see *Further information* on page 49). In addition to mountain weather conditions an avalanche 'risk category' is given. *Category 1* is low risk and 5 is very high. It is vital to understand that the category is a summary of conditions, so for example in *Category 3* conditions some slopes may be highly prone while others are snow-free. It is therefore unwise to rely on this information alone, and essential to collect different information and develop your own judgement and understanding.

SAIS reports are posted in some Scottish newspapers, outdoor shops, ski resorts and outdoor centres. They can also be viewed on the Web (www.sais.gov.uk). As with the weather, it is far more useful to develop a picture of recent events rather than just to have a 'snapshot' single view of the situation. We would recommend that you monitor developments leading up to your planned walk in order to help you make informed decisions.

Dos and don'ts:

- Do check the weather forecast for the day and find out the weather history for the previous days

- Do avoid areas of heavy snow build up for example, by planning to ascend or descend ridges in heavy snow

- Do avoid any slope that you are uncertain about

- Do not assume a path, or set of tracks, follows an avalanche-free route

- Do not assume conditions today will be the same as they were last night

- Do take every opportunity to get to know different types of snow condition

For further information on avalanches see 'A Chance in a Million' by Barton and Wright.

Walking on snow without crampons

When you find yourself on hard snow without crampons, take your time, kick hard and use the edge, toe or heel of the boot to cut into the surface. When crossing slopes you can 'saw' into a hard surface by kicking across the slope with the edge of your boot and you can employ this technique at other times by kicking across the slope even when going straight up. Needless to say this process requires relatively stiff boots. The axe should be held in the uphill hand as it will offer support as you lean into the slope and if the snow is very hard then use your axe to cut steps.

Walking in crampons and when to put them on:

When you first try it, walking in crampons is surprisingly difficult. It is easy to trip up, spike your own leg or tear your gaiters when not used to them. The following tips should help:

- Keep your feet flat to the surface.

- In wet snow, crampons collect compacted snow between the points – this is known as *ball up*. Severe balling up covers the spikes, so do not allow excessive build up by tapping them with the axe to free the snow.

- Develop a walking style where your feet are further apart. Take short steps.

- Avoid baggy overtrousers or loose gaiters which will snag as you walk.

Get used to your crampons on relatively non-testing ground. It is better to stumble and trip on the valley floor on the approach to a hillside, than to find yourself gripped by the unfamiliarity of your footwear when in a potentially serious place.

Mountain Rescue teams report many incidents where a walker has slipped whilst not wearing crampons, but also note that crampons were being carried in the casualties sack. It is easy to delay putting on crampons until they are really needed – at which point it is invariably difficult to put them on! One of the first lessons to learn is to anticipate where you will need your crampons and make sure you have already strapped them to your feet before you reach this point. When you are proficient at putting them on and taking them off, the time saved by being able to move quickly will more than compensate for the time spent putting them on.

Other winter hazards

Frozen and part frozen streams and lakes

In the UK you should avoid walking across frozen water surfaces as it is rarely sub-zero long enough for thick ice to have formed. Getting wet in winter conditions needs to be avoided at all costs.

Self Arrest

An ice axe has many uses: for stability when negotiating tricky steps, for cutting foot-steps on hard snow or ice, to gain purchase in ascent or descent and for self-arrest in the event of a slip.

Be very careful when practising. It is not just the angle of the slope that needs to be right (neither too fast nor too slow), but also the run-out. An ideal slope is one where you could happily slide to a standstill without any self-arrest and with no dire consequences. Practice self arrest on safe slopes and keep doing it until the movement becomes automatic – try to practice 'unexpected' falls by sliding backwards or starting with your eyes closed in order to get disoriented.

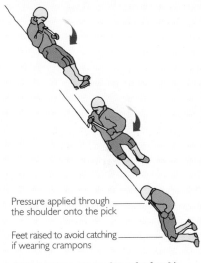

Pressure applied through the shoulder onto the pick

Feet raised to avoid catching if wearing crampons

Self arrest using an ice axe from a feet-first slide on the back

Verglas

Verglas typically develops as the spray from running water freezes onto the ground (particularly rocky surfaces), or because of a very rapid freeze during or after rain. This is extremely slippery and difficult to walk on. The best advice is to try to avoid these areas and learn to recognise when and where they might occur. Sometimes verglas can be so severe that crampons may be required to get up or down the path.

Photo – Courtesy of Craghoppers

Camping off the beaten track at the end of a long day in the hills adds an extra dimension to the hill walking experience. Most wild camping is not strictly legal, though many landowners tolerate it provided that no traces are left. In some cases the landowner will have requested that permission be asked before wild camping.

chapter 6

Camping places fresh demands on the walker and, more importantly, on the environment. A heavier sack must be carried and there is a greater need for self-sufficiency. The following kit list and tips will hopefully be helpful on your next camping trip.

Additional equipment

- Large rucksack
- Tent
- Sleeping bag
- Sleeping mat
- Stove, fuel and matches
- Pans and cutlery
- Water container
- Trowel
- Tent repair kit
- Stove repair kit
- More food

Equipment tips

- Choose a tent which is light, strong and easy to put up. Look for a hard-wearing groundsheet, good ventilation, strong zips and good-quality poles.
- A collapsible water container will save a lot of space.
- Take plenty of matches or lighters and keep them in waterproof containers.

Backpacking tips

- Look to minimise weight with your choice of each item of equipment. Be ruthless with your packing.
- On multi-day trips lay your sleeping bag out to air each morning (assuming it's not raining) before packing it away. This stops it becoming progressively damper.

Other camping tips

- Cook outside the tent or in the porch. This minimises condensation and reduces the risk of burning the tent down.
- Fill your water containers before settling down.

Site selection

- Sheltered if high winds are expected
- Near water
- Flat, soft but dry ground
- Above water table

Camping and the environment

Camping 'wild' and bivvying are very different undertakings from staying at an established campsite. With no facilities at hand you need to think carefully about your impact – both physical and visual. Here are some suggestions.

- Keep your group as small and discreet as possible
- Camp away from roadsides or popular areas – your presence may attract other campers to your unofficial 'site'

Camping – be as discreet as you can to avoid disturbing the environment and other countryside users.

- Be inconspicuous. A brightly-coloured tent can spoil the view, wherever you are. It is best not to leave your tent up during the day when other walkers are likely to pass by.

- Avoid camping at a site for more than a day. If this is unavoidable move the tent every couple of days to let the vegetation under it recover.

- Pitch the tent in a way that avoids having to cut drainage ditches or move boulders. If you do have to move rocks replace them before you leave. Remember – the aim is to leave the site as you found it.

- Litter – plan ahead. If you brought it all in you should be able to take it all out! Carry out all litter – even biodegradable material is slow to decompose in the mountain environment and may be scattered by animals. Do not dig rubbish in or try to hide it under boulders. Also, try to take away any other litter left by people less considerate than yourself.

- Fires are highly destructive. Apart from the fire risk, charred fire sites are unattractive. Moreover, the limited amounts of dead wood in the uplands are essential habitats for the insects on which birds and other animals feed, and for fungi which are an important part of the ecosystem.

- Clean, pure water is a valuable resource relied upon by many people living in the mountains. Feeling clean is great after a day's exercise, but rinsing soap into a watercourse can severely upset the chemical balance of the water. The nutrient content of streams in most upland areas is low, and altering this by adding pollutants could kill local insect and plant life. Question whether it is necessary to take soap and detergent on your trip? If it is, dispose of soapy water well away from water courses. All toilet areas must also be at least 30 metres from running water (see the *Sanitation* section on page 43). Always consider the impact of your actions downstream.

There is a difference between 'wild' camping and 'free' camping. 'Wild' camping in the hills is a very special experience, bringing you as close to nature and wilderness as is possible in the UK. If what you want is to camp free of charge, spare a thought first for the financial problems faced by many hill farmers. Campsite fees will help support them whilst not greatly damaging your pocket.

Staying out in winter: camping and snow holes

In the context of this booklet it is not appropriate to go into detail but the following points may be useful.

An unplanned bivouac in the most severe of winter conditions could have very serious consequences for anyone lacking appropriate knowledge.

Camping on snow

- A good site is even more important than in summer conditions. Consider: what if the wind changes direction? what if it thaws? and so on.

- Compact the snow by walking up and down on it before you pitch the tent.

- Pegs are unlikely to be reliable anchors in snow. Use boulders, ice axes and buried bags of snow.

- Ground insulation is crucial to a good night's sleep. Take a good foam or self-inflating mattress.

- When cooking, avoid having to melt snow as it is slow and uses a lot of fuel. Find running water if you can.

- If you are planning to camp in one place for some time a thin (3mm) foam mat tent underlay improves insulation and protects the ground sheet.

- If possible (winds may make it difficult) keep the tent ventilated at night to reduce condensation.

Improvised shelters: snow holes, trenches & domes

The ability to improvise shelter can be a lifesaver if it is not possible to walk out. In essence this involves simply digging into compact snow to escape from the wind and to create a pocket of still air. Different snow conditions dictate that different types of shelter are constructed and a typical snow hole, which can be dug into a bank of firm snow, is shown opposite. When deciding on a location for a snow shelter, be aware of possible changing conditions – might the wind change direction and strip the slope that you are dug into? Is a thaw forecast? and so on. Remember that the single greatest factor you are trying to escape is exposure to the wind.

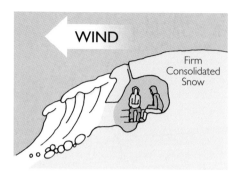

Constructing a snow hole in a drift. The entrance must be cleared of drifted snow throughout the night to ensure adequate ventilation.

Photo – Richard Heap

environment and access

chapter 7

Millions of people enjoy walking in the uplands
of Britain. While our individual impact is usually
minimal, the fact that so many of us are in the
mountains can cause problems – for both the
environment and for other users.

Impact of hill walking

Much can be done to minimise erosion and disturbance by thinking through the implications of our activities and applying common sense:

- Some damage can be easily avoided – such as not running down scree slopes, which leads to rapid erosion of an important ecological habitat.

- Others are less obvious – such as walking within an erosion scar rather than around it, which would enlarge the eroded area.

A badly eroded footpath – avoid making the problem worse.

- Think about your route. For example, much of the initial damage on steep slopes is caused by repeated kicking of steps; try to avoid this by zig-zagging across such slopes.

- While sensible safe footwear is essential for mountain walking, it is both less erosive and more comfortable to wear the lightest footwear that is suitable for the terrain. Is a pair of heavy boots really appropriate for summer walking?

Paths: Paths have been constructed in many areas to protect mountains from the erosion that is caused by the sheer volume of visitors. It is important to use these paths wherever possible, rather than taking shortcuts, which negate expensive and time-consuming footpath work.

Similarly, drainage channels and culverts are essential to take erosive surface water away from paths and should not be blocked or dammed in any way.

Cairns: Some cairns are important landmarks but most are an unnecessary intrusion and detract from the character of a wild and remote setting. Building cairns exacerbates erosion and is the mountain equivalent of graffiti.

Boundaries: Boundaries such as drystone walls, are traditional structures and can be historical features in themselves. Fences are more intrusive but are still very important stock boundaries and are often used for conservation purposes. Boundaries will be damaged by climbing over them – walls are very expensive to repair – and fences are irreparably damaged as soon as the galvanised wire is stepped on. Use stiles and gates wherever possible.

Litter: None of us likes to see discarded wrappers and plastic bottles in the mountains. Take care not to drop any and where possible, remove any that are present. Even apple cores and sandwich crusts are eyesores: orange peel can take twenty years to rot away – take all your litter home.

Access

Mountain landscapes may seem vast and our presence in them inconsequential. However, all land belongs to someone – even 'common land' – and in enjoying access to it we must act in a considerate manner.

Access in theory. Access is all about balancing up the 'Three Rs' – *rights*, *responsibilities* and *restrictions*. Where the right of access is enjoyed this is complemented by responsibilities on users and restrictions to protect landowners' and conservation interests. Successful management of access is where all parties recognise and respect the legitimate interests of others.

And in practice. Where restrictions on access have been imposed these should be the minimum necessary to protect the special interest of the land and must, therefore, be observed. If you disagree with these, contact the organisation involved to discuss the reasons rather than contravening the guidelines. Access may have resulted from years of sensitive negotiation with landowners and others. To ignore restrictions could aggravate a delicate situation or, at worst, lead to access being withdrawn for everyone.

Gates and fences: These are not usually erected to keep people out but to control the movement of stock and prevent overgrazing of sensitive areas. Please leave gates as you found them. Use the gates and stiles provided rather than risk damage by climbing over walls and fences.

Dogs: Dogs cause many problems. Allowing dogs to roam free during the lambing season threatens the lives of sheep and the livelihood of the hill farmer. It is a criminal offence to allow your dog to worry stock, and farmers are legally empowered to shoot any dog that is causing distress to grazing animals. Dogs cause other problems: disturbing wildlife; barking and disrupting other users; defecating near paths or along the bottom of cliffs. Always consider the interests of others who use the land.

Mass organised events: Large events, such as 'challenge' or sponsored events, are increasingly popular as fundraising opportunities. They often involve large numbers of people and can cause significant damage and disturbance to wildlife. Organisers need to consider whether such an event is appropriate in the mountain environment and to plan very carefully. Advice is available from many land managers, such as National Park Authorities, and the National Trust.

The BMC runs a network of regional Access Representatives. They help negotiate access arrangements with landowners and conservation bodies. Please contact the BMC with any information which you think would be valuable for our Access Reps.

Sanitation

There is a reluctance amongst people to talk about what is one of our most natural functions! And yet, in not thinking carefully about this we can endanger human health and potentially poison the mountain environment. Doing either can easily be avoided. Never forego an opportunity to use a proper toilet. If this is not possible, remember some simple guidelines:

Protect fresh water. A mountain stream is a vital source of fresh water for hill farmers and for campers. It will also be a home or water source for wildlife.

- Ensure you are at least 30 metres away from running water when you defecate.

- When camping, defecate downhill from your campsite; collect drinking water from above your camp.

- The smell from urine and excrement are unpleasant. Avoid either in enclosed spaces (caves, ruined buildings and so on), or behind huts.

Leave no trace. There are few things worse than coming across human waste on the mountainside.

- Defecate at least 50 metres from paths and 200 metres from huts.

- Dig a hole 15 cm (6") deep to bury your excrement. If this is not possible, keep well away from paths and spread the excrement thinly to increase the rate of its decomposition (squashing it under a boulder will slow decomposition).

- In snow, dig down into the soil. Give a thought to the consequences when the snow melts!

'Accessories'. Toilet paper and sanitary towels are slow to decompose and may be dug up by animals.

- Burn toilet paper if possible. If there is any fire risk, carry it out. Burying it is the last resort.

- Tampons and sanitary towels should be carried out – plastic screw-top containers are convenient.

Where to 'go' in the great outdoors

43

Carry out techniques. Walkers and climbers in North America are encouraged to carry out all their excrement when they leave a wilderness area. Disposal facilities for removing human waste from the hills in Britain are being developed, but containers remain possible sources of contamination.

For a more comprehensive look at the environment and the mountain walker see the BMC booklet *Tread Lightly*.

Photo – Carl Ryan

Sadly accidents do happen and the consequences will range from the inconvenient to the desperately serious. There is no golden rule for how to act in an emergency but there are some principles that may help.

Accidents & emergencies

In the event of an accident or emergency:

- Don't panic.

- All reasonable efforts should be made to cope with the situation without resorting to rescue services, providing that you do not make any injuries worse than they are already.

- Give spare clothing to the injured person and do your best to provide shelter for them (see *Camping in the Hills* on page 37 for advice on snow shelters).

- If self-help is not possible, then rescue services need to be contacted. Whether this is by mobile phone or landline, the rescue team will need to know where you are and have an idea about the condition of the victim. If you have dialled 999 ask for the police, say which area you are in and say you want mountain rescue.

- If using a mobile keep it switched on after making the call.

- If members of the party need to descend to a landline:

  - Choose a safe route, this might not be the quickest but a second accident must be avoided.

  - Mark the casualties' position on a map and take it along.

Going for help is a relatively easy decision to make if the party numbers four or more. At least two can descend and one can stay with the casualty. If there are only two or three in the group this becomes a more difficult judgement. In such a situation attracting help from others on the hills will greatly help. This is where the whistle and torch come in. The international distress signal is six blasts or flashes followed by a minute's interval and then repeated.

If no local help is forthcoming a decision will have to be made as to whether to leave the casualty alone or (if there are three members of the group) sending a lone messenger. Here the answer can only be arrived at by considering the injury, the conditions and the capabilities of the other members of the party.

Unplanned bivouacs

Whether the result of an injury, a navigational error or unexpected conditions, an unintentional night out is one of those things a walker has to be prepared for. Such nights out are best avoided and realistic planning, headtorches and an early start can all help to avoid them.

If, for whatever reason, you are caught out:

- Shelter from any wind is crucial. A plastic bivouac bag or a fabric bothy bag will be of great help here. On snow, digging a snow hole or trench will make all the difference. More people within a sheltered area will create greater warmth.

- Put your spare clothing on before you get too cold. If possible, remove wet clothing. If you have spare, dry socks put these on.

- Sit on anything that will provide insulation from the ground.

- In severe conditions, keep an eye on other members of the party for signs of hypothermia.

- Come morning, if everyone is fine and if you feel rescue services may have been alerted, try and get word out as soon as possible and put a stop to the search.

First aid

It is beyond the range of this booklet to teach first aid skills. For an individual not practiced in first aid or emergency care there is only so much that can be done for an injured person and this section will try and identify these actions. For further information see the BMC publication *First Aid on Mountains* by Steve Bollen.

The first aid pack

Plasters; sterile wound dressing; elastic adhesive bandage; painkillers (strong and standard if possible); antiseptic wipes, burn dressing; second skin or similar; paper and pencil; salt (for cramp).

Many good commercial kits are available but the kit can equally be built up at the local chemists.

Traumatic incidents

In the event of a serious incident the following, potentially life-saving actions must be addressed in order:

A **Airway-ensure breathing is unobstructed.** Check the tongue and pull it forward if causing a blockage. Clear the mouth of blood or vomit. Remove false teeth.

B **Is the victim breathing?** If not administer mouth to mouth. Breath into (an adult) about 12 times a minute and don't stop until they start breathing for themselves.

C **Circulation – is there a pulse?** Checking the neck pulse is best. If not start immediate cardiac massage (probably at the same time as giving mouth to mouth).

Having followed through the ABC consider the possibility of a head or spinal injury. If the victim is unconscious, assume this and immobilise the neck. If airway obstruction is a problem or there is vomiting then roll the victim carefully into the recovery position. Do what you can to keep the victim warm.

The recovery position

Shock

Shock is common in mountain accidents. Keep the patient warm and reassured, if practicable elevate limbs. Do not overheat.

Bleeding

Control with direct pressure and elevate bleeding limbs.

Broken limbs

Immobilise carefully and give what pain relief you can.

Sprains etc

Usually best to leave the boot on. This gives support and the injured party a reasonable chance of being able to get down with minimal assistance.

Hypothermia (Exposure)

This occurs when the body's core temperature has cooled. Symptoms range from mild confusion, slurring of speech, loss of co-ordination and lethargy to coma. In such a situation, if the cooling is allowed to continue, death will result.

Exposure is usually either the result of poor preparation, such as insufficient clothing or food, wearing wet clothes, exhaustion, or it occurs following an accident. If hypothermia is suspected then treatment should begin immediately.

Treatment revolves around trying to raise the core temperature slowly. If possible, wet clothing should be removed and the victim placed in a warm environment for example, a sleeping bag, if possible wrapped in a space blanket. In extreme conditions it may be necessary for other members of the party to share heat with the victim.

Dehydration is likely so encourage intake of warm fluids.

The **Do Nots** include giving alcohol, rubbing in an attempt to improve circulation and allowing further exertion.

Mountain Rescue in the UK

The UK's voluntary Mountain Rescue teams, like those they assist, are all enthusiastic mountaineers. They are well supported by the excellent RAF teams and emergency services. The rescue service is free of charge and is co-ordinated by the office of the local Chief Constable, except in coastal areas where the Coast Guard has responsibility.

The local voluntary teams are co-ordinated by the Mountain Rescue Council. Funding for the local teams comes from donations, local police authorities, the MOD and grants. The teams are very busy and their time much in demand.

To allow them to do their job, false alarms should be minimised. To this end, please try and follow the relevant advice given in this booklet.

The MRC has set up a series of first aid posts in the hills where emergency equipment is located. For further details on first aid posts and the Mountain Rescue Council see the **Mountain and Cave Rescue Handbook** which is available from the BMC Office.

Photo – Courtesy of Craghoppers

Where to go next?

chapter 9

Books

All of the following titles are available direct from the BMC.

Walking

A guide to hill walking, Chris Townsend (Crowood)

Mountain navigation, Peter Cliff (Cordee)

Mountaincraft and leadership, Eric Langmuir (MLTB)

Tread lightly, (BMC)

Mountaineering and climbing

Climbing rock (BMC)

Crampons (BMC)

Handbook of climbing, Fyffe/Peter (Pelham)

Knots (BMC)

New climbers handbook (BMC)

Ropes booklet (BMC)

First aid

First aid on mountains (BMC)

Weather and hazards

A chance in a million, avalanche safety, Barton & Wright (SMT)

Avalanche safety for skiers and climbers, Tony Daffern (Diadem)

Dealing with water hazards in the mountains, Plas y Brenin

Weather for hill walkers and climbers, Thomas (Sutton)

Videos

The complete winter experience (BMC)

Safety on mountains (BMC)

Magazines

Climber, PO Box 28, Altrincham, Cheshire WA15 8FR

High, 336 Abbey Lane, Sheffield S8 0BY

OTE, PO Box 21, Buxton, Derbyshire SK17 9BR

TGO, Caledonian Magazines, 6th Floor, 195 Albion Street, Glasgow G1 1QQ

Trail, EMAP, Apex House, Oundle Road, Peterborough PE2 9NP

Addresses

BMC

177–179 Burton Road
Manchester M20 2BB

Telephone – 0161 445 4747
Email – office@thebmc.co.uk
Web – www.thebmc.co.uk

Summit magazine
Clubs list
Huts list
Insurance
Information Service

The Mountain Training Boards

MLTB

Siabod Cottage
Capel Curig
Conwy LL24 0ET

Telephone – 01690 720 314
Email – info@mltb.org
Web – www.mltb.org

SMLTB

Glenmore Lodge
Aviemore
Inverness-shire PH22 1QU

Telephone – 01479 861 248
Web – www.glenmorelodge.org.uk

NIMLTB

House of Sport
2a Upper Malone Road
Belfast
Northern Ireland
BT9 5LA

Telephone – 01232 381 222

IMTB (BOS)

House of Sport
Longmile Road
Walkenstown
Dublin 12
Eire

WMLTB

Siabod Cottage
Capel Curig
Conwy LL24 0ET

Telephone – 01690 720 361

UKMTB

Siabod Cottage
Capel Curig
Conwy LL24 0ET

Telephone – 01690 720 272
Email – theukmtb@aol.com
Web – www.ukmtb.org

Scottish Avalanche Information Service

SAIS co-ordinator
Glenmore Lodge
Aviemore
Inverness-shire PH22 1BR

Telephone – 0800 096 0007
Web – www.sais.gov.uk

Ramblers Association

1/5 Wandsworth Road
London SW8 2XX

Email – ramblers@london.ramblers.org.uk
Web – www.ramblers.org.uk

McofS

4a St Catherine's Road
Perth
Scotland
PH1 5SE

Telephone – 01738 638 227
Web – www.mountaineering-scotland.org.uk

McofI

House of Sport
Longmile Road
Dublin 12
Republic of Ireland

Telephone – 00353 1 400 7376
Email – mci@eircom.net
Web – www.mountaineering.ie

The National Centres

Plas y Brenin National Mountain Centre

Capel Curig
Conwy LL24 0ET

Telephone – 01690 720 214
Email – info@pyb.co.uk
Web – www.pyb.co.uk

Glenmore Lodge

Aviemore
Inverness-shire PH22 1BR

Telephone – 01479 861 256
Web – www.glenmorelodge.org.UK

Tollymore

Tollymore Mountain Centre
Bryansford
Newcastle
Co.Down BT33 0PT
Northern Ireland

Telephone – 028437 221 58
Web – www.tollymoremc.com

Tiglin

The National Mountain and Whitewater Centre
Devils Glen Forest
Ashford
County Wicklow

Telephone – 01686 430 630

British Mountain Guides

Siabod Cottage
Capel Curig
Conwy LL24 0ET

Telephone – 01690 720 386
Web – www.bmg.org.uk

Mountain Bothies Association

Ted Butcher
26 Rycroft Avenue
Deeping St. James
Peterborough PE6 8NT

Web – www.ma.hw.ac.uk/mba/

Long Distance Walkers Association

Bank House
High Street
Wrotham
Kent TN15 7AE

Web – www.ldwa.org.uk

Other useful websites

Association of Mountain Instructors

www.fachwen.org/ami/

Meteorological office

www.meto.govt.uk

BMC

Insurance you can trust

10 reasons to choose BMC insurance

- Simple and easy to purchase
- Immediate professional service
- Worldwide 24 hour helplines
- 10 point customer service charter
- 3 day to annual cover
- UK, Europe or Worldwide cover
- Cover available for many sports including hill walking, trekking, climbing, and skiing
- Medical, search and rescue, repatriation and baggage cover come as standard with no hidden extras
- Comprehensive and excellent value for money

Contact us today for a copy of your BMC Travel and Activity Insurance Guide

Over 50,000 **hill walkers, climbers and mountaineers put their trust in the British Mountaineering Council to provide expert advice, services and information on the outdoors. BMC insurance is designed by experts to give you reassurance and peace of mind wherever you travel. All our quality policies are designed free from unreasonable exclusions or restrictions. What's more all surpluses from BMC services are invested in work that promotes your interests and protects your freedoms – so the only one to profit is you.**

Instant cover
Online or by phone

website: www.thebmc.co.uk
tel: **0161 445 4747**
email: **insure@thebmc.co.uk**
fax: **0161 445 4500**

**BMC
Member Services
FREEPOST MR9759
Manchester M20 7AD**

BMC

  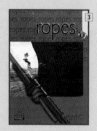

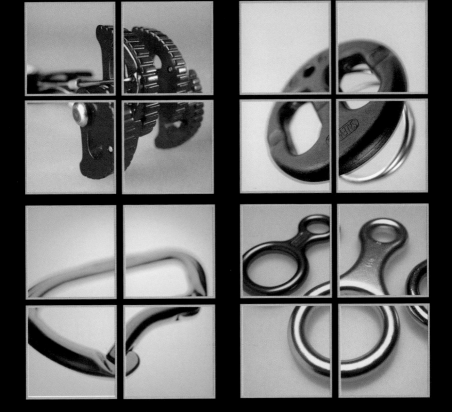

BMC
Membership Options

Join the BMC today for a full range of benefits including: insurance, news, training events, *Summit Magazine* and, for under 18's, *gripped?* magazine.

Individual Membership

- Individual Member
- Individual Member with *High* or *On the Edge* magazine
- Individual Member with *High* and *On the Edge* magazine

Family Membership*

- Family Membership
- Family Membership with *High* or *On the Edge* magazine
- Family Membership with *High* and *On the Edge* magazine

* Family membership includes up to 2 adults and 3 children living at the same address. Reduced membership for under 18's, full time students and the unemployed.

Join online now at www.thebmc.co.uk